JOHN G. ROBERTS, JR.

John G. Roberts, Jr.

Chief Justice

Lisa Tucker McElroy

Lerner Publications Company · Minneapolis

For my wonderful daughter, Abigail Diana McElroy, who would love to dress up in judicial robes someday. May all your dreams come true!

Photographs are published with the permission of: © J. Scott Applewhite/Getty Images, pp. 2, 35; © Jim Watson/AFP/Getty Images, pp. 6, 31; Courtesy of the Roberts family, pp. 8, 9, 10, 13, 21, 25, 26, 27, 28, 29; © La Lumiere H.S./ZUMA Press, pp. 11, 12; © Atlantic Photo Service/Courtesy of Special Collections Department, Harvard Law School Library, p. 15; © Fabian Bachrach/Courtesy of Special Collections Department, Harvard Law School Library, p. 17; © Liaison/Getty Images, p. 18; Courtesy Ronald Reagan Library, p. 19; Photographs by Tracey Atlee, p. 23; © Chris Kleponis/ZUMA Press, p. 33; © Joe Raedle/Getty Images, p. 34; © Alex Wong/Getty Images, p. 37; © Jason Reed/Reuters/ CORBIS, p. 39.

Front Cover: © R. Strauss/ZUMA Press.

Text copyright © 2007 by Lisa Tucker McElroy

Lerner Publications Company
A division of Lerner Publishing Group
241 First Avenue North
Minneapolis, MN 55401 U.S.A.

Website address: www.lernerbooks.com

Library of Congress Cataloging-in-Publication Data

McElroy, Lisa Tucker.
    John G. Roberts, Jr. : chief justice / by Lisa Tucker McElroy.
       p.   cm. — (Gateway biography)
    Includes bibliographical references and index.
    ISBN-13: 978-0-8225-6389-1 (lib. bdg. : alk. paper)
    ISBN-10: 0-8225-6389-4 (lib. bdg. : alk. paper)
    1. Roberts, John G., 1955- —Juvenile literature. 2. Judges—United States—Biography—Juvenile literature. 3. United States. Supreme Court—Biography—Juvenile literature. I. Title. II. Series.
    KF8745.R6M43 2007
    347.73'2634—dc22
                                          2006000244

Manufactured in the United States of America
1 2 3 4 5 6 – BP – 12 11 10 09 08 07

CONTENTS

President Bush announces his nomination of John G. Roberts, Jr., as an associate justice of the the Supreme Court during a televised speech on July 19, 2005.

The night of July 19, 2005, was hot and muggy in Washington, D.C., and the media lights made it even warmer. The clicking cameras sounded like crickets chirping. Standing off to the side, John Roberts's wife held their children's hands. The president said, "Tonight I am honored to announce that I am nominating [John Roberts] to serve as an associate justice of the Supreme Court."

Americans watched with interest as the vibrant young lawyer with kind eyes was nominated as a justice of the U.S. Supreme Court. But the story was not yet over. Six weeks later, John Roberts's mentor, Chief Justice William H. Rehnquist, died. Even as the president joined Americans in mourning the former chief justice, he offered them a view of the future. He and John Roberts faced the cameras again. "It is fitting," Bush said, "that a great chief justice be followed in office by a person who shared his deep reverence for the Constitution, his profound respect for the Supreme Court and his complete devotion to the cause of justice."

One month later, on September 29, 2005, John Glover Roberts, Jr., lawyer, judge, husband, and father of two, became the seventeenth chief justice of the United States.

GROWING UP

John ("Jackie") Glover Roberts, Jr., was born on January 27, 1955, in Buffalo, New York. He was the only son and the second child of John Glover Roberts, Sr., an executive for a steel company, and Rosemary Podrasky Roberts, a homemaker. In addition to his older sister, Kathy, John would later have two younger sisters, Peggy and Barbara.

When John was eight years old, the Roberts family moved to Long Beach, Indiana. Long Beach is a beautiful town on the tip of Lake Michigan. The family was very traditional and close-knit. They ate dinner together every night and said grace at the beginning of the meal.

John and his sisters especially loved summers in Long Beach. John biked everywhere on his Sting-Ray bike with a banana seat and bell. For

John *(right)* and his sister Kathy

As a young boy, John Roberts was known as Jackie. When he was eleven, though, he realized that the only Jackie he'd heard of was Jackie Kennedy (the former First Lady). So he asked to be called John.

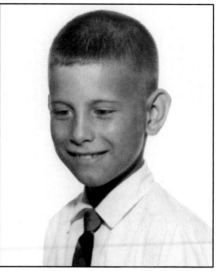

the town's Fourth of July parade, the Roberts kids decorated their bikes and rode down the town's main street. All of the local kids loved riding through the hilly streets and trails in their neighborhood. The Roberts kids also played in town-organized softball and kickball leagues. Of course, they went swimming at the lake. They were usually gone from morning until night!

All of the Roberts kids liked skateboarding, and they also taught themselves to water-ski. They had a boat, but the starter didn't work very well. They got to know the Coast Guard very well! Usually, John drove the boat and the girls water-skied behind. And in the colder weather, their favorite activity was sledding on Bump Hill, a summer sand dune that turned into a slippery, snowy hill in winter.

During the school year, all of the Roberts children attended Notre Dame Elementary School in Long Beach. Even though the Indiana winters were cold, there was no school bus, so they had to walk the mile to school and back.

On winter evenings, Rosemary and Jack did not allow the children to talk on the phone or watch television after 7:00 P.M. Instead, the children had to do their homework. When it was done, the Roberts family played Monopoly and Scrabble together. John also liked to put together model airplanes.

Jack and Rosemary Roberts always cared about their family. The children were not allowed to fight or argue, although they had their share of childhood mishaps. For example, when John was sixteen or seventeen, he forgot to pick Barb up from ice-skating. She waited so long for him that her toes got frostbitten! Another time, when John was twelve, he mowed over a hornet's nest when

John and his sisters *(from left to right)* Kathy, Barbara, and Peggy

mowing the lawn and was stung a hundred times.

But the story the family loves best about John was his earliest try at lawyering. His mother remembers that John got into trouble in fourth grade for throwing an orange at a wall. When the principal called him in, John explained. "I didn't mean to hit the wall. I threw the orange at Timmy O'Donnell's head, but he ducked. That's why the orange hit the wall. It's Timmy's fault." The principal and John's mother bought it.

GOING TO BOARDING SCHOOL

In ninth grade, John began high school at La Lumiere School in nearby La Porte, Indiana. Although he boarded at the then all-boys school, he often went home on the weekends.

At La Lumiere, John was a student leader. He served on the student council. He sang in the choral group and acted in drama club

The chief justice *(third from left, in background)* enjoyed his role as Peppermint Patty in a high school production of *You're a Good Man, Charlie Brown.*

John (number 21) played football at La Lumiere. This picture appeared in the 1973 yearbook.

productions. Although he has been known to call himself a "slow-footed halfback," he was captain of the football team. He was a student leader who lived in the dorm to help advise younger students. His teachers and friends remember that the other students looked up to John. He was well liked and respected by all.

But where John really shone was in the classroom. His wrestling coach, David Kirkby, remembers him as the best student ever to attend La Lumiere. His roommate, Robert McLaverty, agrees. "If I burned the midnight oil, John was up until 2:00 A.M. . . . he pushed himself very hard for someone who was so smart." In fact, John often went above and beyond on assignments. His wrestling coach remembers that for a class presentation, John read a seven-volume set on philosophy and dressed in a bedsheet toga like Socrates to talk to his fellow students. Kirkby suspects that if the bell hadn't rung, John Roberts would still be talking.

At La Lumiere, John won the science fair with his automatic table fork project. He also became a National Merit Scholar. Never one to brag, he did not tell his parents that he'd won the scholarship. Instead, they read about it in the paper. When his mother scolded him, he replied, "Mom, you would have told everyone!" John also made his parents proud by working summers to help pay for his education.

John completed most of his required course work in three years, so he spent his last year of high school doing independent studies. When he graduated in 1973, he was first in his class.

John's La Lumiere Class of 1973 senior year portrait

COLLEGE AND LAW SCHOOL AT HARVARD

As the top La Lumiere grad, Roberts earned admission to Harvard College. Cambridge, Massachusetts, is a long way from Indiana, but Harvard is a first-rate university with many opportunities for learning.

John Roberts loved his college experience. He especially enjoyed meeting many other bright young men and women from around the country. He also liked his major. Says the chief justice, "In studying world history, I was very wide-eyed. I was a kid from a small town learning about a much bigger world. It was exciting." Roberts remembers, "I had a wonderful professor for a course about Samuel Johnson [English author of the 1700s]. He brought the era to life."

> Yo-Yo Ma, the famous cellist, was in John Roberts's college class.

At Harvard, Roberts lived with other students in a dorm called Leverett House. He did not continue playing football or singing, though, choosing to concentrate on his studies. His focus paid off. In 1976 John Roberts graduated summa cum laude (with highest honors). He completed all of his course work in just three years.

Then it was on to Harvard Law School, where Roberts was an instant star. His friend, Richard Lazarus, remembers, "He was so smart that some other students thought that they just weren't cut out for law school.

Then they realized that they were fine. He was just way ahead of the rest of us."

At first, Roberts did not intend to practice law. He still liked history, but he knew that there were not many jobs for historians. Because he was interested in legal history, he thought that he might pursue a career in teaching law.

But Roberts came to love the law. During his three years at Harvard Law School, he changed his mind and decided to become a practicing lawyer. He worked very hard in his job as managing editor on the *Harvard Law Review*, a magazine published by top Harvard students.

The *Harvard Law Review*'s staff photo from the 1978–1979 school year. Roberts is in the fourth row, fifth from the left.

"Even after he was gone," says Evan Slavitt, who would serve on the *Law Review* a few years later, "everyone remembered what a great, careful job John Roberts had done. We all tried to be like him."

At Harvard Law School, Roberts also made some good friends, who would later encourage and support him in his career. One reason that his friends were loyal was that they knew John to be very fair. Although he and his friends sometimes disagreed on politics, Roberts looked at issues from every side.

A FAIR AND JUST OUTLOOK

Ask anyone about John Roberts, and they'll say, "He's the nicest guy you'd ever want to meet." Press them, and they'll add, "and one of the smartest."

In fact, his law colleagues say that he's humble, funny, thoughtful, and sincere. One has commented, "He is a brilliant man. . . . His personal integrity is above reproach. . . . He is the kind of person you would want to have lunch with. . . . This is a person I really trust."

John supports others in their views, even when he disagrees. "It's a quality that John still has today," says his sister Peggy. "He says that you can disagree without being disagreeable. He can understand many points of view, and he has friends in other political parties. He's not someone who says, 'It's my way or the highway.'"

In 1979 John Roberts graduated magna cum laude from Harvard Law School. He then began what would be a remarkable career.

CLERKSHIPS IN THE FEDERAL COURTS

The next two years would be exciting ones for Roberts. Because of his near-perfect law school record, he had the opportunity to serve as a law clerk to two federal court judges. Law clerks work with judges as apprentices, usually for one year.

Roberts's first clerkship was in New York City. He worked in the chambers of Judge Henry J. Friendly, a judge on the U.S. Court of Appeals for the Second Circuit. As an appellate judge, Judge Friendly's job was to review decisions of the federal trial courts. As his law clerk, Roberts's job was to help the judge write

Judge Friendly was one of Roberts's early mentors in the practice of law.

William H. Rehnquist preceded John Roberts as chief justice of the United States, serving from September 1986 until his death in 2005.

opinions and think about cases. He remembers this as a wonderful time in his life. He loved thinking about the law, and he respected Judge Friendly's approach to cases.

But the best was yet to come. After clerking for Judge Friendly, Roberts received what many recent law graduates consider to be the ultimate honor. In 1980 he accepted a job to clerk for William H. Rehnquist, then an associate justice on the U.S. Supreme Court in Washington. For the next year, John Roberts spent almost every waking moment either in the justice's chambers or walking with the justice around the neighborhood, talking about cases. He learned a great deal from Rehnquist. He would always consider the justice to be a mentor and friend.

PRE-COURT CAREER

The next several years flew by. Roberts began his Washington career working as a lawyer in the U.S.

government. First, he was a special assistant to the U.S. attorney general. Then he worked as one of President Reagan's lawyers in the White House. After a few years in high government positions, he joined a Washington law firm, Hogan & Hartson. There, he represented clients from many different backgrounds and viewpoints. The firm made him a partner in 1988.

The following year, another interesting opportunity came along. Roberts was asked to become principal deputy solicitor general, a job in which he represented the U.S. government before the U.S. Supreme Court and in other federal courts. He was to learn from and enjoy this job for the next four years.

Roberts worked as a lawyer for the White House when this photo with President Reagan *(left)* was snapped in 1983.

While he was working in the solicitor general's office, he experienced one of the few disappointments of his career. President George H. W. Bush nominated Roberts to serve on the U.S. Court of Appeals for the District of Columbia Circuit. Roberts and his family were honored and thrilled. Unfortunately, however, it was not to be. Although Roberts was qualified for the job, the nomination died in committee. He was very disappointed, say friends, but not discouraged. He decided to use the next years of his career to learn and grow as a lawyer and contribute to the legal community.

In 1993, with the swearing in of Democratic president Bill Clinton, the political party in power changed. John Roberts, a Republican, chose to return to Hogan & Hartson. He practiced law there for the next ten years. During these years, he earned the respect of all his colleagues. Remembers Patricia Brannan, his law school classmate and Hogan & Hartson partner, "John was a wonderful colleague. He treated everyone with great respect and gave people his time."

Although Roberts himself was very busy with his appellate law practice—he would eventually argue thirty-nine cases before the Supreme Court, between his government and private practices—he always

JOHN ROBERTS LIKES LOTS OF MUSIC, but he especially enjoys listening to John Sousa marches. When he was a lawyer, he played the marches on his way to argue cases before the Supreme Court.

found time to help others with their cases too. Roberts also did a great deal of pro bono work, or legal work for clients who could not afford to pay.

John Roberts was a big success. Says Patricia Brannan, "John succeeded everywhere and was happy everywhere."

After some years at Hogan & Hartson, another dream came true. In 2001 President George W. Bush nominated Roberts to become a judge on the U.S. Court of Appeals for the District of Columbia Circuit. A great many Washington lawyers, Democrats and Republicans alike, supported his nomination in a letter to the Senate. They praised his "unquestioned integrity and fair-mindedness." Although it took a while, finally, in 2003, the Senate unanimously voted to confirm him. He would serve for

Chief Justice Rehnquist *(left)* swears in Roberts *(right, with wife, Jane)* as a judge for the U.S. Court of Appeals in 2003.

two years, during which Roberts says, he "felt very blessed and fortunate to be on the Court of Appeals."

MARRIAGE AND FAMILY

For many years, John Roberts worked so hard that he did not have much time for dating. All of that changed in the summer of 1991, when he and ten friends rented a beach house in Dewey Beach, Delaware.

One Saturday in August, John Roberts met Jane Marie Sullivan for the first time. She was also a Washington lawyer. Jane had received her bachelor's degree in 1976 from the College of the Holy Cross. She received a master's degree in education from Melbourne University in 1977 and her M.S. from Brown University in 1981. She graduated from Georgetown University Law Center, J.D., in 1984. John and Jane talked for hours on the beach, mostly about their families, and enjoyed each other's company. Sullivan was especially attracted to Roberts's terrific sense of humor.

Unfortunately, however, they could not start dating right away. Jane Sullivan went to work in Australia for fifteen months and did not return to the United States until the spring of 1993. Luckily, though, the two met again that autumn at a dinner party. At the party, they found themselves talking the evening away. From that point on, they dated seriously. Soon they fell in love.

John Roberts and Jane Sullivan married in a beautiful Catholic ceremony at Saint Patrick's in Washington, D.C.

Their wedding in the summer of 1996 was quite an event! After a short engagement, John Roberts and Jane Sullivan were married by Monsignor Peter Vaghi. They both remember the beauty of the ceremony, the magnificent cake, and the enthusiastic conga dancing at the reception. Their large families and all of their friends attended and celebrated.

Now both in their early forties, John and Jane Roberts sought to grow their family through adoption. Both thought that adoption was a wonderful way to become parents, and their families supported them completely.

As is often the case, the adoption process turned out to be long and difficult. Even though the Roberts qualified early on to adopt a child, there were several disappointments.

A few years passed. The couple continued to hope and believe that a child would come their way. Finally, in the summer of 2000, they received good news from their adoption agency. A birth mother had chosen them to adopt her baby.

The Roberts were thrilled! They could hardly wait to become parents. Knowing that soon they would have little time as a couple, they decided to take a vacation to Canada. For several days, they relaxed in a remote area away from phones and computers.

When they went to the airport to fly home, however, they realized that they had several missed calls on their cell phones. Another adoption agency had called. "We have a baby for you. Can you come and get her?" the agency said.

They could hardly believe it. They were going to have two children—one right away and another in four months! They flew to the area where the birth mother lived and met their newborn daughter. They named her Josephine Marie Sullivan Roberts, after John's grandmother, JoJo, and Jane's godmother, Josephine O'Brien Cassidy.

ADOPTION IN THE ROBERTS FAMILY

If you ask John Roberts to name the greatest moment of his life, he answers, "The birth of my two children." Adopting Josie and Jack changed his life completely. "The children are the joy of our lives," he says. Even becoming chief justice of the United States is no big deal, he says, "when you compare it to the feeling of holding your children for the first time."

Josie and Jack know that they are adopted, and they identify with other adopted children. They even read picture books about adoption.

Both the Sullivan and Roberts families rejoiced when Josie and Jack joined the family. Both families threw parties when the babies came home for the first time. The baptisms of both children *(Jack's baptism below)* were important family events.

Jack would like his parents to go back to the adoption agency and get him a little brother!

John and Jane Roberts spend their first Christmas with Jack *(in his father's arms)* and Josie *(in her mother's arms).*

The Roberts were delighted with their new role as parents. They hardly had a chance to get settled, though, before John (Jack) Glover Roberts III came along a few months later. It took a lot of energy to care for two infants. But the couple felt that Josie and Jack made their family complete.

THE CHIEF JUSTICE and his family have several pets: two goldfish, Cleo and Rocky; two unnamed snails; and a ladybug named Dora.

John and Jane Roberts became very involved parents. Every morning he makes the children breakfast and packs their lunches. She helps them get dressed. Every weekend they attend church with the children. If the children behave well in church, they are allowed to play soccer afterward in their church clothes.

27

THE CHIEF JUSTICE cooks Mickey Mouse-shaped waffles and bacon for his wife and children on Saturday mornings.

When Josie and Jack started school, their parents attended their various activities. Always the student, John

Josie adjusts her father's "costume" on Halloween 2005.

especially enjoys helping the children with their home-work assignments. For example, in pre-kindergarten, Josie received an assignment to do a report on Neptune. Roberts helped her research the planet and make a model out of a Styrofoam ball. One Thanksgiving, Jack's class disguised paper turkeys so that hunters couldn't find them. His father helped Jack costume his turkey as a pirate, complete with a gold belt and black hat with skull and crossbones.

Both John and Jane Roberts remain very close to their parents and siblings. His parents and two of his sisters live nearby. They regularly hold family events such as bap-tisms, weddings, birthday parties, and holiday dinners.

In the summer John and Jane Roberts rent a beach house and invite the entire extended family. All of the Sullivans and Robertses spend time together. They relax on the beach, fly kites, canoe, and kayak. Everyone takes

Although his favorite sport is golf, John Roberts loves kayaking!

The Roberts family gets into the Easter spirit in this 2003 photo. John and Jack stand behind *(from left to right)* Grandpa Roberts, Aunt Peggy, Josie, and Grandma Roberts.

turns cooking. John's grilled fish and shrimp marinara are always in high demand!

THE NOMINATIONS

If you had asked me to put on a piece of paper a list of the five people . . . who most deserved this, based on quality and excellence and brilliance, I would put him on that list.
    −Patricia Brannan, Hogan & Hartson partner
      and John Roberts's law school classmate

John Roberts has devoted his entire professional life to the cause of justice and is widely admired for his intellect, his sound judgment and his personal decency.
    —George W. Bush, July 19, 2005

He's important! He wears a robe!
    —Jack Roberts, four-year-old son of John Roberts

John Roberts would have been happy to work for the rest of his career on the U.S. Court of Appeals. He found his job there to be interesting and fulfilling. His wife and young children brought him much pleasure. He even got in an occasional game of golf! Of course, he watched with interest the happenings at the Supreme Court. But being nominated to serve on the Court when Associate Justice Sandra Day O'Connor announced her retirement was a welcome but unanticipated surprise.

It happened in July of 2005. Like many other judges and lawyers on the president's "short list," Roberts met with the president's advisers early in the month. They asked him many questions, and he told them he would be willing to serve if asked. Then, considering a nomination to be a "long shot," according to his friend Robert McLaverty, Roberts went to London to teach a law course there.

It was the middle of the night in London when Roberts got the call. Would he fly back to Washington? The president needed to speak with him. Telling only his assistant and his wife, Roberts did so. But then, at 12:35 in the afternoon on July 19, he sat in his study and talked by phone with the president. He hung up the phone, then told his wife to get ready. In just a few hours, the president would announce the nomination of John G. Roberts, Jr., to be an associate justice of the Supreme Court.

Both John and Jane remember that the next few hours were a whirlwind. John went directly to the White House. Jane and the children joined him there a few hours later for dinner with the president and the First Lady. The first dogs attended too, much to Josie and Jack's delight!

At 9:00 that evening, the president introduced John Roberts to the nation. Jack danced, Josie smiled shyly,

President Bush introduces Roberts as his nominee for the Supreme Court on July 19, 2005.

and the whole world watched. Justice O'Connor, who was on a fishing trip when the announcement came, approved. "He's first rate," she said.

But John had to convince the Senate, which would vote on his nomination. For the next few months, John met as many senators as he could. "Every day was a different chapter," says Roberts. "It was a very busy time." In addition to meeting the senators, Roberts spent a great deal of time getting ready for his confirmation hearings. The hearings were set to begin after Labor Day at the beginning of September. Roberts remembers, "During this time, my conversations with the president were very encouraging and supportive. He made me feel very good about taking on the responsibility."

But the whirlwind would increase. On the Saturday before Roberts's hearings were to begin, his mentor, Chief Justice William H. Rehnquist, died of cancer. Two days later, on September 5, the president announced that John Roberts was his choice to fill the chief justice spot.

The confirmation hearings were postponed by a week. Soon, however, they began, with Roberts's wife, children, sisters, and parents in proud attendance. Josie and Jack accepted a bribe to behave from Monsignor Vaghi, the

THE CHIEF'S FAVORITE MOVIES are *Dr. Zhivago* and *North by Northwest*. In fact, he told the Senate about them during his Supreme Court confirmation hearings.

Roberts testifies during his confirmation hearings.

family priest. If they were good, said the priest, they could have two scoops of ice cream afterward. Jack being Jack, he negotiated. "Three!" he said, holding up three fingers. "Done!" said Monsignor Vaghi. And behave they did, charming all the senators present. Monsignor Vaghi paid up: Josie enjoyed three scoops of chocolate ice cream, while Jack had vanilla.

At the hearings, some senators were concerned that Roberts's political views might sway his decisions as a justice. Roberts assured them that the opposite was true. "I will remember that it's my job to call balls and strikes and not to pitch or bat." In the end, the senators viewed him just as his colleagues had: fair, smart, and committed to public service. On September 29, 2005, by a vote of 78–22, they confirmed John G. Roberts, Jr., as the seventeenth chief justice of the United States.

FIRST DAYS ON THE COURT

Immediately after the Senate's vote, John Roberts took the oath of office. His wife, Jane, proudly held the Bible on which the new chief justice rested his hand. John Paul Stevens, the most senior associate justice, administered the constitutional oath.

AT FIFTY John Roberts is the youngest chief justice since John Marshall. Chief Justice Marshall was forty-five when he was confirmed in 1801.

Roberts takes the oath of office as chief justice of the United States. He is sworn in by Acting Chief Justice John Paul Stevens *(right)* as Jane Roberts and President Bush *(left)* look on.

Jack whispers in his father's ear before Roberts takes his seat on the Supreme Court bench on October 3, 2005.

Then it was time to get to work! Roberts was confirmed just four days before the Supreme Court term began on the first Monday of October. The new chief spent a good deal of time in his office that weekend, studying the briefs for the arguments in the week to come.

And, of course, his new colleagues helped him out. Each of the other eight justices stopped by to say hello once the chief was settled in his chambers. The chief remembers that all of the justices helped him adjust to his new job. They gave him good advice about how the Court worked.

Luckily, in some ways, the Court felt quite familiar. "It hasn't changed too much in the twenty-five years since I clerked," the chief says. "Arguments are held at the same time, everyone sits in their familiar chairs behind the bench. Justice Stevens was a justice when I was a law clerk."

On Monday, October 3, 2005, the new Supreme Court term began with the official installation of John Glover

Roberts, Jr. After the ceremony, John Roberts took the bench for the first time as chief. "It was a very happy moment," he says. "I was very honored to be part of the institution."

THE SUPREME COURT

The Supreme Court is sometimes called the Highest Court in the Land. Its job is to decide legal issues involving the U.S. Constitution and laws passed by the U.S. Congress. The issues decided by the Supreme Court affect everyone living in the United States, even kids!

The Supreme Court hears cases in the Supreme Court building across the street from the Capitol Building in Washington, D.C. The building, where the justices also have their chambers, is open to public tours. Visitors may attend oral arguments, but the arguments are not televised.

In addition to Chief Justice Roberts, the Supreme Court has eight associate justices, most of whom have served on the Court for many years. Seven are men, and there is one woman. To be on the Supreme Court, a lawyer or judge must be nominated by the president and confirmed by the Senate. Once he or she is confirmed, a Supreme Court justice serves for life or until retirement. John Roberts may be chief justice for thirty years or more!

To learn more about the Supreme Court, look for books in the library or visit www.supremecourtus.gov, the Court's website.

A typical day in the chief justice's chambers is very busy. Most days, John Roberts leaves his house at about 7:30 A.M. He pulls into the Court's basement parking lot and says hello to the police officers. Then he rides the elevator up to his chambers on the first floor. He pours a cup of coffee and goes down to the Court cafeteria to get a muffin (much to the surprise and delight of the people who work in the cafeteria!).

Then the chief justice gets to work. He checks his e-mail and confers with his assistants. As he drinks his cup of coffee, he often talks with his law clerks. Then he looks over any cases scheduled for oral argument (an opportunity for a lawyer to tell the Court about her case) that day.

Roberts *(right)* shakes hands with Samuel Alito *(left)*. Alito joined the Supreme Court after Sandra Day O'Connor retired in 2005.

Several days each month, the Supreme Court holds oral arguments. Just before the arguments are to begin, a buzzer sounds to let the justices know that they need to get ready. When he hears the buzzer, John Roberts goes to the justices' robing room and puts on his robes. He shakes hands with each of the other justices before they all take the bench.

After oral arguments, the chief justice meets the other justices for lunch in the justice's dining room. He enjoys talking with them about court-related matters, but they often talk about other things too.

RUMOR HAS IT that John Quincy Adams died on the leather couch currently in the chief justice's chambers. Because there's an identical couch in the Capitol, no one is sure which couch is the real thing.

JUDICIAL ROBES

William H. Rehnquist, the sixteenth chief justice and John Roberts's predecessor, wore gold stripes on the sleeves of his judicial robe for many years. When John Roberts became chief, many wondered whether he would wear the stripes too. After much thought, however, he decided not to. Says the chief, "You have to earn your stripes, and I thought it was a little early to be doing that . . . it seemed to me that simple black was more appropriate." Quips the chief, "On the other hand, no one ever looks to me for fashion advice!"

Roberts poses for an official photo with the eight associate justices of the Supreme Court. They are *(front row, left to right)*: Antonin Scalia, John Paul Stevens, Roberts, Sandra Day O'Connor (now retired and replaced in 2005 by Samuel Alito), Anthony M. Kennedy *(back row, left to right)*, Ruth Bader Ginsburg, David H. Souter, Clarence Thomas, and Stephen G. Breyer.

The chief likes to hear about Justice Ginsburg's most recent visit to the opera, for example, or about a great football game someone attended.

In the afternoons, the chief reads and writes about the law. He reads briefs, or complicated papers that lawyers send the Court about their cases. He writes opinions, or long explanations on how a case should be resolved and why. During argument weeks, he and the other justices meet often in conference. The conference is a closed, confidential meeting in which the justices discuss what cases the Court should hear. They also discuss their views on cases they have already heard.

In nonargument weeks, the chief justice might travel to give speeches or judge law school competitions. Of course, as these weeks are calmer around the Court, they are a good time for him to work on administrative matters. As chief justice, he is responsible for overseeing the Supreme Court building and the hundreds of employees who work there. What's more, he is in charge of all of the federal courts in the United States, and he helps advise courts in foreign lands. One of his favorite responsibilities is being chancellor (ceremonial director) of the Smithsonian, the wonderful museums in Washington, D.C. "It's fascinating to figure out how I can contribute," he says.

BEING CHIEF JUSTICE

Indeed, says Roberts, this opportunity to contribute cannot be matched. He marvels at the importance of the Supreme Court's work, even in the most ordinary cases. He sees the existence of the Court as an amazing achievement. "To have a system where people can come and talk about problems and resolve them under the law instead of by force is a rare accomplishment in world history and in the world today. I am proud and grateful to be a part of it."

And, he says, as he begins this next stage of his career, "People before me have worked very hard to make this institution. I want to carry it forward. It's a heavy responsibility. I'm going to roll up my sleeves and get on with it."

THE CHIEF JUSTICE'S MESSAGE TO CHILDREN

"It's hard to aspire to be a Supreme Court justice," says Chief Justice Roberts. However, children should appreciate that they can be involved in the legal system. Kids who are interested in becoming lawyers should understand that there are all different kinds of lawyers and law practices.

"For example," says the chief, "[former] Justice O'Connor was a member of the Arizona legislature, and Justices Ginsburg and Breyer taught law on the East Coast. Justice Souter was a government lawyer in New Hampshire, and Justice Stevens was a lawyer in private practice in Chicago." Supreme Court justices come from all parts of the country—the chief grew up in Indiana—and from all kinds of personal and professional backgrounds. The chief justice reminds kids, "Remember that you can follow many paths."

More Fun Facts about John Roberts

- The chief justice's favorite color is green.

- Josie and Jack Roberts were the first young children of the Court in many years. When their dad was confirmed as chief justice, the Supreme Court Marshal's office had to buy car seats so they could ride in the Court SUV with their dad.

- John Roberts loves chocolate. His assistants keep the chambers' candy dish stocked with Hershey's Kisses, and he regularly helps himself. When he was in law school, he ate chocolate chip ice cream at the same ice cream shop every single day. His sister Peggy baked him chocolate chip cookies before his Supreme Court confirmation hearings.

- The chief justice often travels with his family. He enjoys hiking in New Zealand and Canada and visiting his wife's family cottage in Ireland.

- Before John Roberts was confirmed, students at his high school held mock confirmation hearings. Although they didn't take a vote at the end, it sure seemed like the students would have voted to confirm him. They liked him a lot!

- On the November 15, 2005, broadcast of *Jeopardy!* John Roberts was the subject of a two-hundred dollar question in the Government and Politics category. Alex Trebek gave the answer, "On Sept. 29, 2005, John Roberts was sworn in as this." The correct question? "What is the chief justice of the United States?"

IMPORTANT DATES

1955	John Glover Roberts, Jr., born in Buffalo, New York
1973	Graduates first in his high school class from La Lumiere School
1976	Graduates from Harvard College summa cum laude
1979	Graduates from Harvard Law School magna cum laude
1979–80	Clerks for Judge Henry J. Friendly, U.S. Court of Appeals for the Second Circuit
1980–81	Clerks for William H. Rehnquist, then-associate justice of the Supreme Court
1981	Becomes special assistant to the U.S. attorney general
1982	Becomes associate counsel to the president, White House Counsel's office
1986	Joins Washington law firm, Hogan & Hartson

1989	Becomes principal deputy solicitor general, U.S. Department of Justice
1992	Nominated to the U.S. Court of Appeals for the District of Columbia Circuit; nomination lapses in committee
1993	Rejoins Hogan & Hartson
1996	Marries Jane Marie Sullivan
2000	Becomes a father with the adoption of Josephine Marie Sullivan Roberts and John Glover Roberts III
2001	Name resubmitted to the U.S. Court of Appeals for the District of Columbia Circuit
2003	Confirmed to the U.S. Court of Appeals for the District of Columbia Circuit
2005	Nominated on July 19 to replace Sandra Day O'Connor as an associate justice of the Supreme Court of the United States
	Nominated on September 5 to replace William H. Rehnquist as chief justice of the United States
	Sworn in on September 29 as the seventeenth chief justice of the United States

SOURCE NOTES

Unless otherwise noted, all direct quotes derive from a series of interviews between the author, Chief Justice John G. Roberts, Jr. (November 8, 2005, and November 17, 2005), Rosemary Roberts (November 23, 2005), Peggy Roberts (November 17, 2005, and multiple dates thereafter), Kathleen Roberts Godbey (November 21, 2005), Barbara Roberts Burke (November 21, 2005, and December 21, 2005), Jane Sullivan Roberts (November 14, 2005, and multiple dates thereafter), Richard Lazarus (December 21, 2005), and Diane Nelson (December 30, 2005).

p. 7   "Bush: 'A Man of Extraordinary Accomplishment'" *CNN.com*, July 19, 2005, http://www.cnn.com/2005/POLITICS/07/19/bush.roberts.transcript/index.html (March 28 2006).

p. 7   Ibid.

p. 12   Robert McLaverty, "Profile of Supreme Court Nominee John Roberts," C-SPAN, August 23, 2005.

p. 16   Evan Slavitt, interview with author, January 16, 2006.

p. 16   Patricia Brannan, "Profile of Supreme Court Nominee John Roberts," C-SPAN, August 25, 2005

p. 20   Ibid.

p. 21   Ibid.

p. 21   Letter to Senators Daschle, Hatch, Leahy, and Lott from members of the Bar of the District of Columbia, Executive Session, Nomination of John G. Roberts, Jr., to be Chief Justice of the United States, S10529-05, 109th Cong., 1st sess., *Congressional Record* 151 (September 28, 2005).

p. 29   Patricia Brannan, "Profile of Supreme Court Nominee John Roberts," C-SPAN, August 25, 2005.

p. 30   "Bush: 'A Man of Extraordinary Accomplishment'" *CNN.com*, July 19, 2005, http://www.cnn.com/2005/POLITICS/07/19/bush.roberts.transcript/index.html (March 28 2006).

p. 30   Robert McLaverty, "Profile of Supreme Court Nominee John Roberts," C-SPAN, August 23, 2005.

p. 32   Sandra Day O'Connor, *CBSNews.com*, July 20, 2005, http://www.cbsnews.com/stories/2005/ 07/20/politics/main710487.shtml (March 14, 2006).

p. 42   *Jeopardy!*, episode 4872, first broadcast November 15, 2005, by King World.

FURTHER READING

No other biographies of John Roberts for young readers exist at this time. The following websites include interesting information about John Roberts:

The Justices of the Supreme Court
    http://www.supremecourtus.gov/about/biographiescurrent.pdf

The White House
    http://www.whitehouse.gov/infocus/judicialnominees/roberts.html

ACKNOWLEDGMENTS

Special thanks to Chief Justice John G. Roberts, Jr., who participated with enthusiasm in this project; Diane Nelson, Laverne Frayer, and Janet Tramonte in the chambers of the chief justice; Steve Petteway in the Supreme Court curator's office; Jane Sullivan Roberts; Rosemary Roberts, Peggy Roberts, Kathleen Godbey, and Barbara Burke; Professor Richard Lazarus, Georgetown Law School; Don Scherer; Nnamudi Amobi, for his excellent research assistance; Dean Robert Ward, at the Southern New England School of Law; Judge Francis Larkin; Tom Goldstein; Tracy Atlee, the Roberts's wedding photographer; Kirby Hanson, Reagan Foundation; the Ronald Reagan Library; Suzanne Stone, Sr. Researcher, *Jeopardy!;* Jean Reynolds, Jessica Puckett, and Beth Johnson, a fantastic editorial team.

INDEX

Page numbers in *italics* refer to illustrations.